Te Amo, Bebé, Little One

by Lisa Wheeler

Illustrated by Maribel Suárez

LITTLE, BROWN AND COMPANY

New York ❧ An AOL Time Warner Company

Also by Lisa Wheeler:
Porcupining
Bubble Gum, Bubble Gum

For my amigas, Hope Vestergaard and Alicia Gomez Terrel. Te amo…twice!
—L.W.

A mis little ones, Bimba, Pavis y Tebis.
—M.S.

Text copyright © 2004 by Lisa Wheeler
Illustrations copyright © 2004 by Maribel Suárez

First Edition

Library of Congress Cataloging-in-Publication Data

Wheeler, Lisa.
 Te amo, bebé, little one / by Lisa Wheeler ; illustrated by Maribel Suárez—1st ed.
  p. cm.
 Summary: In rhyming verse with Mexican imagery and a Spanish refrain, a mother repeatedly says how much she loves her baby.
  ISBN 0-316-61410-6
  [1. Mother and child—Fiction. 2. Love—Fiction. 3. Stories in rhyme.] I. Suárez, Maribel, 1952–ill. II. Title.

PZ8.3.W5663Te2004
[E]—dc21   2002043638

10 9 8 7 6 5 4 3 2 1

SC

Manufactured in China

The illustrations for this book were done in watercolor on Fabriano paper.
The text was set in Maiandra, and the display type is Le Chat Noir and Zinjaro.

Once upon a springtime morn,
a bouncy, brown-eyed babe was born.
As baby wriggled in the bed,
Mama cuddled close and said:

I love you once. I love you twice.
I love you more than beans and rice.
I love you more than rain or sun,
Te amo, bebé, little one.

As sweet camellias came in hue,
the cactus bloomed…
and baby grew.

Once upon a summer noon,
a cheerful, chubby baby crooned.
As baby cooed an ocean song,
Mama splashed and sang along:

I love you once. I love you twice.
I love you more than beans and rice.
I love you more than sea or sun,
Te amo, bebé, little one.

Atop the waves of turquoise blue,
time sailed on...
and baby grew.

Once upon a country fair,
fiesta music filled the air.
Baby laughed as Mama swayed.
They swirled as mariachis played:

I love you once. I love you twice.
I love you more than beans and rice.
I love you more than earth or sun,
Te amo, bebé, little one.

As autumn's first cool breezes blew,
the palm trees danced...
and baby grew.

Once upon a winter night,
beneath la luna, smiling bright,
a cozy chair rocked to and fro,
keeping time to words sung low:

I love you once. I love you twice.
I love you more than beans and rice.
I love you more than moon or sun,
Te amo, bebé, little one.

In sleepy fields of midnight blue,
the cattle dreamed...
and baby grew,

And grew,
    and grew,
        and grew some more…

and one day toddled out the door.

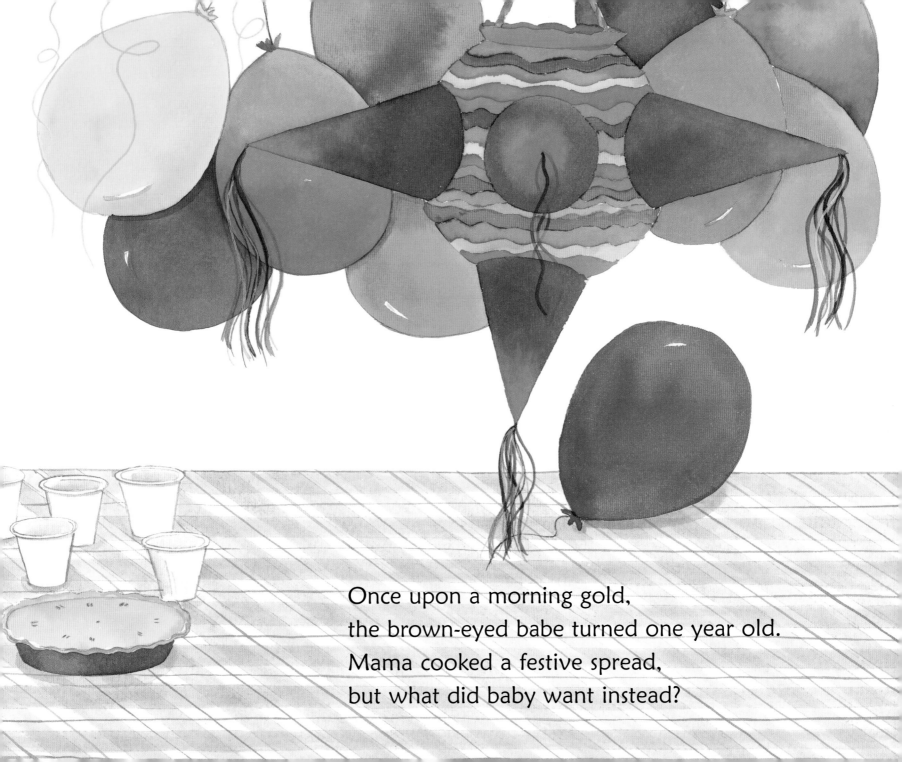

Once upon a morning gold,
the brown-eyed babe turned one year old.
Mama cooked a festive spread,
but what did baby want instead?

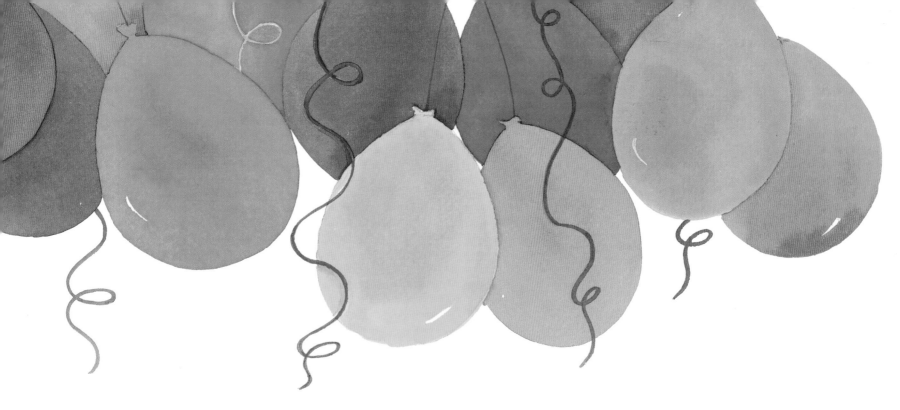

No cakes,
no pies,
no punch with ice...

that baby wanted beans and rice!

I love you once. I love you twice.
I love you more than beans and rice.
I love you more than stars or sun,
Te amo, bebé, little one.